Country ABCs

ITALY ABCs

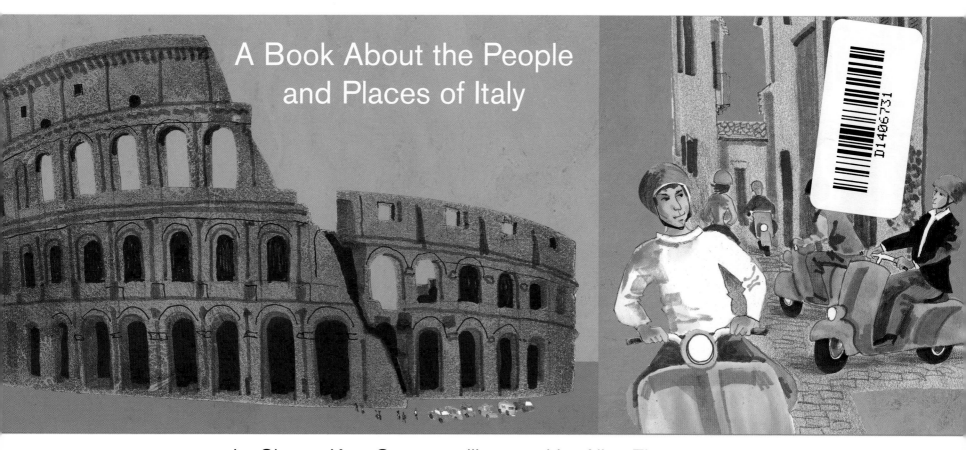

A Book About the People
and Places of Italy

by Sharon Katz Cooper ~ illustrated by Allan Eitzen

Special thanks to our advisers for their expertise:
Elisabetta Assi, Esq.
Italian Academy for Advanced Studies in America
Columbia University in the City of New York

Susan Kesselring, M.A., Literacy Educator
Rosemount–Apple Valley–Eagan (Minnesota) School District

PICTURE WINDOW BOOKS
Minneapolis, Minnesota

Editor: Jill Kalz
Designer: Nathan Gassman
Page Production: Tracy Kaehler
Creative Director: Keith Griffin
Editorial Director: Carol Jones
The illustrations in this book were created in acrylics.

Picture Window Books
151 Good Counsel Drive
P.O. Box 669
Mankato, MN 56002-0669
877-845-8392
www.picturewindowbooks.com

Printed in the United States of America.

 All books published by Picture Window Books
are manufactured with paper containing at least
10 percent post-consumer waste.

Library of Congress Cataloging-in-Publication Data
Cooper, Sharon Katz.
Italy ABCs : a book about the people and places of Italy /
by Sharon Katz Cooper ; illustrated by Allan Eitzen.
p. cm. – (Country ABCs)
Summary: An alphabetical exploration of the people,
geography, animals, plants, history, and culture of Italy.
Includes bibliographical references and index.
ISBN-13: 978-1-4048-1569-8 (hardcover)
ISBN-13: 978-1-4048-1920-7 (paperback)
1. Italy–Juvenile literature. 2. Alphabet books. [1. Italy.
2. Alphabet books.] I. Eitzen, Allan, ill. II. Title. III. Series.
DG417.C65 2006
945–dc22   2005021815

Buongiorno! (bohn-JOOR-no)

People in Italy use this word to say "Good day!" Italy is a country in Europe. It borders Switzerland, France, Austria, and Slovenia. It is a country well known for its ancient cities and beautiful art.

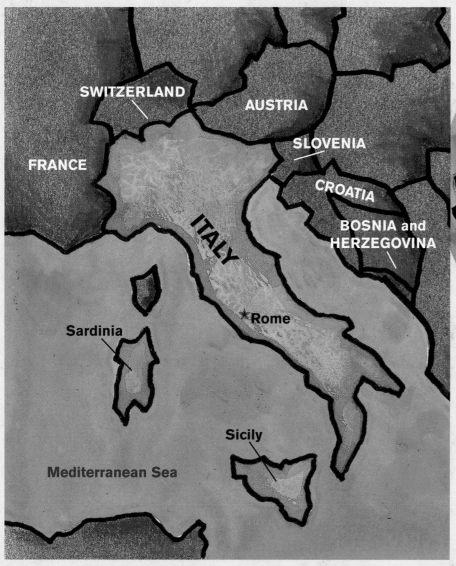

FAST FACT: More people vacation in Italy than live there. Close to 60 million tourists visit Italy every year. Italy's population is about 57 million.

A is for art.

Italy is a world center for art and artists. One of the most famous paintings in the world, Leonardo da Vinci's *Mona Lisa*, comes from Italy. So does Michelangelo's sculpture *David.* Painters such as Leonardo da Vinci, Michelangelo, Sandro Botticelli, and Raphael called Italy their home.

FAST FACT: Michelangelo was both a sculptor and a painter. He painted the ceiling of the Sistine Chapel.

B is for boot-shaped.

On a map, Italy looks like a boot sticking out into the Mediterranean Sea. The boot is surrounded by water. The Tyrrhenian Sea lies to the west, the Adriatic Sea to the east, and the Ionian Sea to the south.

FAST FACT: It's easy to see why Italy is a favorite vacation spot for beach-lovers. Italy has 4,700 miles (7,520 kilometers) of coastline!

Adriatic Sea

ITALY

Tyrrhenian Sea

Ionian Sea

C is for Carnevale (kar-neh-VAHL).

Italians love festivals. The biggest festival of the year is called *Carnevale*. It takes place in February, in Venice, right before Lent begins. It is a colorful event, with people dressing up in costumes and wearing masks.

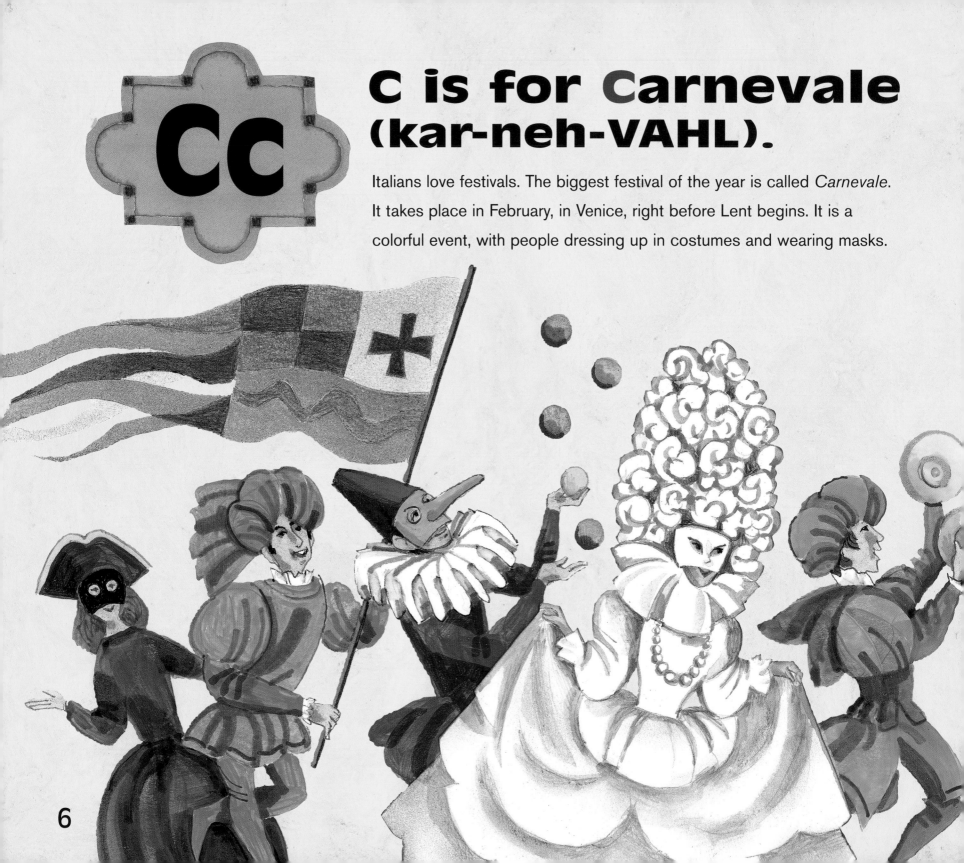

Dd D is for dolce (DOHL-chay).

The word *dolce* means "sweet" in Italian. When a musician plays a piece of music, this word tells him or her to play softly. Italy is home to many famous composers and singers. It is also the world's center for opera, a kind of musical play. Operas first became popular in Italy in the 1600s.

FAST FACT: Even though operas are now performed in many different countries, they are almost always sung in Italian.

7

E is for Etna.

Ee

Mount Etna is one of Italy's active volcanoes. It is about 11,000 feet (3,337 meters) tall, but it changes its height slightly as lava erupts, hardens, and then crumbles. Mount Etna is on the island of Sicily.

FAST FACT: Some people call Mount Etna the "friendly giant" because its lava moves very slowly. People who live at the foot of Mount Etna usually have plenty of time to escape without getting hurt.

Ff

F is for flag.

The Italian flag is green, white, and red. Green stands for hope, white stands for faith, and red stands for charity. Italians have flown this flag since 1796 as a symbol of freedom and togetherness.

9

G is for gelato (jeh-LAH-toh).

Gelato is Italian ice cream. It is made from whole milk, eggs, sugar, and flavoring or fresh fruit. It comes in many flavors, including strawberry, lemon, and chocolate. A shop that sells gelato is called a *gelateria* (jeh-LAH-teh-REE-ah).

FAST FACT: Another Italian treat is *granita* (grah-NEE-tah; frozen ice water in many different flavors).

H is for Holy See.

The Holy See is also called the Vatican. The Vatican is the center of the Roman Catholic religion and the home of the Pope. The Pope is the leader of the Roman Catholic Church. Vatican City is actually a country, even though it is only one small city inside Italy. Most Italians are Catholic.

FAST FACT: Swiss guards protect Vatican City. They wear colorful uniforms designed long ago by Michelangelo.

I is for island.

Italy includes two large islands called Sardinia and Sicily. Sardinia is very mountainous. It lies just south of Corsica, an island belonging to France. Sicily is the island at the "toe" of Italy's "boot." It is the largest island in the Mediterranean Sea.

FAST FACT: Sardinia is known for its hearty bread, seafood, and salty cheese. Sicilian food favorites include eggplant recipes, pizza cooked in a wood-burning oven, and cannoli, a deep-fried pasta tube filled with cheese.

Sardinia

Mediterranean Sea

Sicily

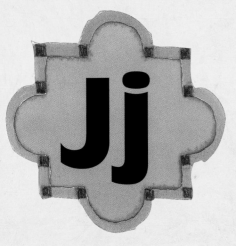

Jj

J is for Julius Caesar.

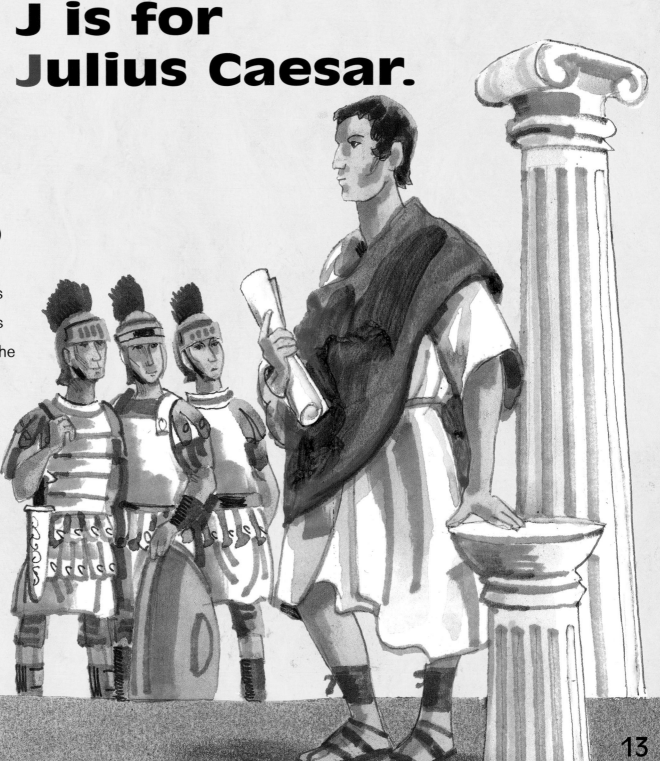

Julius Caesar (100–44 B.C.) was one of the greatest warriors in history. He led his troops into battle many times and won many victories for the Roman Empire. In 46 B.C., Caesar was named Emperor of Rome. But many people thought Caesar had too much power. Because of this, members of his own government later killed him.

13

K is for kingdom.

Rome

Venice

Until about 150 years ago, Italy was made up of two kingdoms. One was the Kingdom of Sardinia (northern Italy), and the other was the Kingdom of Naples (southern Italy). Rome and Venice were independent cities. In 1861, all of them united to become the Kingdom of Italy.

Naples

Sardinia

14

FAST FACT: Rome became the capital of Italy in 1871.

L is for Leonardo da Vinci.

Leonardo da Vinci (1452–1519) was the world's first "Renaissance" man–a person who was good at many different kinds of work. He was an artist, mathematician, scientist, and inventor. He painted the *Mona Lisa* and *The Last Supper*, two of the world's most famous paintings.

FAST FACT: Leonardo da Vinci sketched many of his inventions in his notebooks. He even had ideas for modern-day machines such as airplanes.

15

M is for Mediterranean.

The Mediterranean Sea is quite shallow and warm. It was formed by melting glaciers at the end of the Ice Age, nearly 2 million years ago. The Mediterranean makes the climate of nearby countries such as Italy and France warm and mild.

N is for Naples.

N n

Naples is Italy's third largest city. It is a center for industry and culture. Many tourists visit Naples to see the stone arch called Porta Capuana (below), the National Museum of Archaeology, and the Palazzo Reale (Royal Palace).

O is for olives.

About half of Italy's land is used for farming. Olive trees grow well on the country's sloping fields. Italians make and export olive oil, which is a main ingredient in most Italian cooking.

FAST FACT: Italy also grows many grapes. The juice is used to make wine.

18

Pp

P is for Pisa.

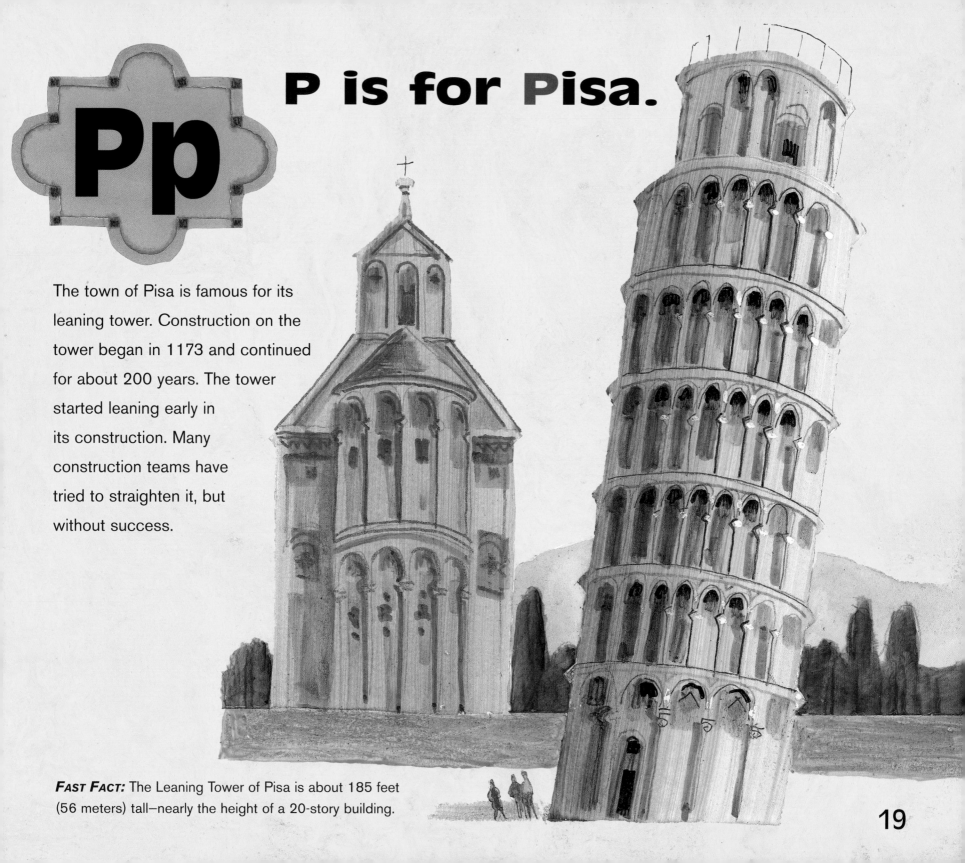

The town of Pisa is famous for its leaning tower. Construction on the tower began in 1173 and continued for about 200 years. The tower started leaning early in its construction. Many construction teams have tried to straighten it, but without success.

FAST FACT: The Leaning Tower of Pisa is about 185 feet (56 meters) tall—nearly the height of a 20-story building.

Q is for quanto (KWAN-toh).

Qq

The word *quanto* means "how much" in Italian. For many years, Italians used the lira as their unit of money. In 2002, they adopted the euro. The euro is the common money for almost all member countries of the European Union.

R is for Rome.

Rome is the capital of Italy. It has been a city for 3,000 years. Today, almost 3 million people live there. Rome has many famous buildings and monuments, such as the Coliseum (below), the Pantheon, Trevi Fountain, and the Roman Forum, a collection of ruins dating back to 600 B.C.

FAST FACT: According to legend, a pair of twins named Romulus and Remus founded the city of Rome.

Ss

S is for scooters.

Motor scooters are a common way to get around on narrow Italian streets. Scooters are like small motorcycles. They are a very popular form of transportation for people of all ages.

T is for Tuscany.

Tuscany is a region of western Italy. It is known for its rolling hills, cypress trees, and rows of grape vines. People in Tuscany use grapes to make a special kind of wine called Chianti (kee-AHN-tee).

FAST FACT: The regions of Tuscany, Marche, and Piedmont grow expensive mushrooms called truffles. White Piedmont truffles can cost up to $1,500 per pound (.45 kilograms)!

U is for universities.

Uu

Italy is home to many old, well-respected universities. The University of Bologna was founded in the 11th century and is the oldest university in Europe. The University of Rome was founded in 1300.

FAST FACT: The astronomer Nicolaus Copernicus studied at the University of Bologna in the 1400s. He was one of the first people to believe that the planet Earth went around the sun.

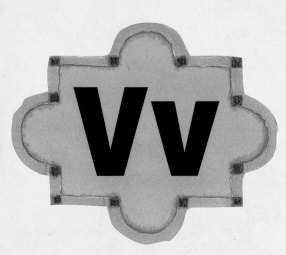

Vv

V is for Venice.

Venice is one of Italy's most unusual cities. It is actually made up of 118 tiny islands. Its streets are canals filled with water. To get around, people travel in small, narrow boats called gondolas.

FAST FACT: Venice has about 400 bridges connecting its many islands.

W is for wolves.

Wolves once roamed through much of Italy. But by 1970, just 100 remained. Most had died either because farmers shot them or because cities grew and destroyed the animals' habitat. Luckily, laws now protect the wolves. Today, there are about 400 wild wolves living in Italy's Apennine Mountains.

FAST FACT: The Alpine ibex lives in the mountains along the France-Italy border. The ibex is a wild goat with large, twisted horns. Its horns were once thought to bring good health.

X is for exports.

Xx

Italian products are sold throughout the world. Italy is especially famous for its fine leather shoes, handbags, olive oil, wine, and fancy sports cars.

Fast Fact: Italy produces the most expensive and recognized sports cars in the world, including the Maserati, Lamborghini, and Ferrari brands.

27

Yy

Y is for yarn.

Italy makes beautiful, high-quality yarns from wool, cotton, and acrylic. These yarns are woven into clothing items such as scarves, sweaters, and mittens.

Z is for ziti (ZEE-tee).

Today, pasta is eaten around the world, but the Italians invented it. There are many shapes of pasta, and each has its own name. Ziti is tube-shaped. Spaghetti is string-like. Ravioli are little pockets that can be stuffed with cheese, meat, or vegetables.

Zz

FAST FACT: Italians also invented pizza—a favorite food of millions of people around the world.

Italy in Brief

Official name: Republic of Italy

Capital: Rome

Official language: Italian

Population: 58 million

People: mostly Italian

Religion: mostly Roman Catholic; small groups of Protestants, Jews, and Muslims

Education: Children are required to go to school until age 14; 80 percent continue through high school.

Major holidays: New Year's Day (January 1), Epiphany (January 6), Easter (March/April), Labor Day (May 1), Republic Day (June 2), Ferragosto (August 15), All Saints' Day (November 1), Christmas Day (December 25), St. Stephen's Day (December 26)

Transportation: trains, cars, scooters

Climate: People inland experience cool winters and mild summers, while those along the Mediterranean have mild winters and hot summers.

Area: 116,303 square miles (301,230 square kilometers)

Highest point: Mont Blanc (Monte Bianco), 15,543 feet (4,710 meters)

Lowest point: Mediterranean Sea, sea level

Type of government: republic

Most powerful government official: prime minister, also called President of the Council of Ministers

Major industries: tourism, machinery, iron and steel, chemicals, food processing, textiles, motor vehicles, clothing, shoes, ceramics

Natural resources: coal, mercury, zinc, marble, asbestos, pumice, natural gas and oil, fish, farmland

Major agricultural products: grapes, beets, soybeans, grain, olives, beef, dairy products, fish

Chief exports: engineering products, textiles and clothing, production machinery, cars, food

Money: euro

Say It in ITALIAN

hi . . . . *ciao* (CHOW)

good-bye . . . . *arrivederci* (ah-ree-vah-DAYR-chay)

please . . . . *per favore* (pear fah-VOH-ray)

thank you . . . . *mille grazie* (MEE-LEE GRAH-tsee-ay)

yes . . . . *si* (SEE)

no . . . . *no* (NOH)

one . . . . *uno* (OOH-nah)

two . . . . *due* (DOO-ay)

Glossary

astronomer–a person who studies stars, planets, and other objects in space

charity–giving to others

composers–people who write music

culture–a set of beliefs and customs shared by a group of people

European Union–a group of 25 countries in Europe that work together

glaciers–large sheets of slow-moving ice

lava–melted rock that oozes or is thrown from a volcano

Lent–the 40 days during which Christians prepare for Easter

mathematician–a person who studies math

To Learn More

At the Library

Fontes, Justine. *A to Z Italy*. Danbury, Conn.: Children's Press, 2004.

Peterson, Christine. *Italy: A True Book*. Danbury, Conn.: Children's Press, 2000.

Powell, Jillian. *What's It Like to Live in Italy?* Columbus, Ohio: Waterbird Books, 2003.

On the Web

FactHound offers a safe, fun way to find Web sites related to this book. All of the sites on FactHound have been researched by our staff.

1. Visit *www.facthound.com*
2. Type in this special code: 1404815694
3. Click on the FETCH IT button.

Your trusty FactHound will fetch the best sites for you!

Index

LOOK FOR ALL OF THE BOOKS IN THE COUNTRY ABCS SERIES:

Australia ABCs
Brazil ABCs
Canada ABCs
China ABCs
Costa Rica ABCs
Egypt ABCs
France ABCs
Germany ABCs
Guatemala ABCs
India ABCs

Israel ABCs
Italy ABCs
Japan ABCs
Kenya ABCs
Mexico ABCs
New Zealand ABCs
Russia ABCs
The United States ABCs
Venezuela ABCs
Vietnam ABCs